OUT OF BONDAGE

A Fall To Grace

Randy Dodge

Copyright © 2017 by Randy Allen Dodge

Out of Bondage
A Fall to Grace
by Randy Allen Dodge

Printed in the United States of America.

ISBN 9781498497503

All rights reserved solely by the author. The author guarantees all contents are original and do not infringe upon the legal rights of any other person or work. No part of this book may be reproduced in any form without the permission of the author. The views expressed in this book are not necessarily those of the publisher.

Unless otherwise indicated, Scripture quotations taken from the New King James Version (NKJV). Copyright © 1979, 1980, 1982 by Thomas Nelson, Inc. Used by permission. All rights reserved.

Scripture quotations taken from the New American Standard Bible (NASB). Copyright © 1960, 1962, 1963, 1968, 1971, 1972, 1973, 1975, 1977, 1995 by The Lockman Foundation. Used by permission. All rights reserved.

www.xulonpress.com

Dedication

This book is dedicated to my Lord and Savior without whom there is no purpose, and to my son, Isaiah, my pride, and my daughter, Julia, my joy, and to the faithful unsung heroes of the faith who prayed me back into fellowship.

TABLE OF CONTENTS

Dedication v
Acknowledgments xi
Introduction xiii

Week One: Grace Not Works 15
    Day 1: Grace and Truth 17
    Day 2: Doing and Being 19
    Day 3: Renewing Your Mind 21
    Day 4: Whitewashed Tombs 23
    Day 5: Grow in Grace and Knowledge 25
    Day 6: Self-Righteousness 27
    Day 7: Balance Between Faith and Works 29
Week Two: Finally Free 31
    Day 1: Sowing and Reaping 33
    Day 2: Use the Whole Armor of God 35
    Day 3: Being Transformed 37
    Day 4: Surrender Brings True Freedom 39
    Day 5: Obedience Brings Freedom 41
    Day 6: Doing God's Will Brings Freedom 43
    Day 7: Knowing God Is in Control Brings Freedom 45

Week Three: Delight, Commit, and Trust ... 47
- Day 1: Trust God with ALL Your Heart ... 49
- Day 2: The Paul and Silas Solution ... 51
- Day 3: Refreshing From His Presence ... 53
- Day 4: Commit Your Way to Him ... 55
- Day 5: Victory in Jesus ... 57
- Day 6: Accountability Is a Must! ... 59
- Day 7: What if You Miss the Mark? ... 61

Week Four: A Call to Sexual Purity ... 63
- Day 1: The Prodigal Son ... 65
- Day 2: The Horrible Pit of Sin ... 67
- Day 3: Prayer and Fasting ... 69
- Day 4: Take Up Your Cross Daily ... 71
- Day 5: Refuse the Victim Mentality ... 73
- Day 6: Trust God to Fulfill Every Need ... 75
- Day 7: The Act of Repentance ... 77

Week Five: Resisting Temptation ... 79
- Day 1: Dealing with Pride ... 81
- Day 2: Dealing with Deception ... 83
- Day 3: Take My Yoke upon You ... 85
- Day 4: Don't Let Your Guard Down ... 87
- Day 5: Exercise Godliness ... 89
- Day 6: Get an Attitude Adjustment ... 91
- Day 7: A Warning ... 93

Week Six: Damaged by Divorce ... 95
- Day 1: God's Perfect Will ... 97
- Day 2: The God of Reconciliation ... 99
- Day 3: Remarriage? ... 101
- Day 4: Dealing with the Scars of Divorce ... 103

Table of Contents

    Day 5: Not Damaged, Not Lacking. 105
    Day 6: Comforted to Comfort. 107
    Day 7: Transparent Testimony 109

Conclusion: The Forty-Day Fast 111
Appendix 1: My Testimony 121
Appendix 2: Other References 135

Acknowledgments

All the credit for this book goes to God, my Lord and Savior, Jesus Christ, and the Holy Spirit, for the blessed Trinity have all been active in my redemption, restoration, and sanctification. Though I am using my life story in prayerful hopes of warning others, this book is not about me it is all about Him. As a believer, I stumbled and He alone kept me from falling into the abyss of forgetfulness. He alone lifted me up and set my feet upon the Rock while putting a new song in my mouth (Psalm 40:2-3).

Introduction

And the prayer of faith will save the sick,
and the Lord will raise him up.
And if he has committed sins, he will be forgiven.
-James 5:15

When a believer falls, this is the time they need the love of the body of Christ. It is not our job to judge the heart or motives when a fellow believer falls, but to reach out in love with one hand extended in grace and the other upholding truth.

My passion is for those alienated from the world around them by their new birth, but shunned by their kindred for the habitual failures that they hate. Satan has sifted them, sin has ravaged them, the world has deceived them, and their own flesh has mocked them. They need to know the truth that God loves them and the healing power of His grace.

This book is about my recovery from multiple addictions. None of them are pretty, all are destructive, and many will have consequences until Christ comes back or I go home to be with Him. My prayer is God will use my transparency and willingness to be open about my shame to warn others. I pray they gain wisdom from my failures and turn from the errors of their ways, for then their souls shall be spared death and a multitude of sins will be covered.

Brethren, if anyone among you wanders from the truth,
and someone turns him back, let him know
that he who turns a sinner from the error of his way
will save a soul from death and cover a multitude of sins. (James 5:19-20)

Week One
Grace Not Works

*Even so then, at this present time
here is a remnant according to the election of grace.
And if by grace, then it is no longer of works;
otherwise grace is no longer grace.
But if it is of works, it is no longer grace;
otherwise work is no longer work.*
-Apostle Paul in Romans 11:5-6

Grace is so simple yet so profound that many of us miss it. Even those of us who get it for salvation and walk in it for a while find ourselves tangled back up again in works.

Like those Christians in Galatia the Apostle Paul addressed in his epistle, we begin to think we can earn favor with God by keeping certain rules and regulations. It seems to be the natural inclination of man, which is why so many stumble at salvation. We think how can anything of any worth be free? Salvation is completely free to us, but it cost God His only Son whose precious life's blood and substitutionary death paid the full price for our sins.

Finally, at the age of twenty-two I understood that part because I also realized there was nothing I could ever do to earn salvation.

If I was going to be saved, I knew God was going to have to do it. Then I had to learn how to live a life that balances grace and works.

Day 1
Grace and Truth

*And of His fullness we have all received,
and grace for grace. For the law was given through Moses, but grace and
truth came through Jesus Christ.*
-John 1:16-17

For me, like so many others, all was well for years after my salvation. I read my Bible daily, had a quiet time with the Lord, memorized and meditated on scripture, attended all church services and functions, and truly grew in knowledge. Unfortunately, I grew much faster in knowledge than I did in understanding grace.

I also found it to be much easier to be doing things for God than being something for God. To be something for God is to hold the truth in one hand while extending grace with the other.

You can memorize truth, but you have to learn grace and that comes by experience and practicing His presence in every aspect of your life.

Read John 3:16-18.
 How much does God love you?

What did He do to prove His love for you?
Why did Jesus give His life for You?

Read Romans 10:9-10.
What must you do to be saved?
Will you make that confession today?

Begin to Journal what you are learning as you begin this walk of discovering both truth and grace.

Day 2
Doing and Being

"A new commandment I give to you, that you love one another; as I have loved you, that you may love one for another. By this all will know that you are my disciples, if you have love for another."
-Jesus to His disciples in John 13:34-35

Like many other Christians, I became so busy **doing something** for God I did not take the time to **be something** for God. Doing something is easy and showy. God may get the glory as He should, but we often bask in the recognition of what we can accomplish for God. I know I did.

God wants us to be holy like He is holy (1 Peter 1:15-16). He also wants us to love one another because others will recognize us as His disciples when we do. It sounds simple. Be holy, be loving, show grace, and speak His truth, but we all seem to fall so very short.

Even after the Holy Spirit came to indwell believers on a permanent basis on the day of Pentecost giving us His divine nature (2 Peter 1:3-4), we do not measure up. Why?

Maybe it is because we fail to avail ourselves of His grace. I believe that is where I fell short.

Read 2 Peter 1:3-4.
Why do we need His divine power working in and through us?
How do we get this power?

Read John 13:34-35.
What will allowing His grace to work in and through us show others about us?
Why is this so important?

Day 3
Renewing Your Mind

"These people draw near to Me with their mouth, and honor Me with their
lips, but their heart is far from Me.
In vain they worship Me, teaching as doctrines the commandments of men."
When He had called the multitude to Himself,
He said to them, "Hear and understand:
Not what goes into the mouth defiles a man;
but what comes out of the mouth, this defiles a man."
-Jesus in Matthew 15:8-11

I expected everyone to be perfect (even though I knew I was not). I expected others to perform certain ways, follow a certain code, wear certain clothing and hair style, have similar music tastes, and so on. That was the legalist in me making me no different than the Pharisees of Christ's day. I became one of the blind leaders of the blind sensing the emptiness, but too proud to admit it.

Many of us are blind in this spot because we forget it is a transformation that starts inwardly. We forget is an on-going **life-long process of being transformed** from glory to glory by His Spirit **to become like Him** (2 Corinthians 3:18).

"And do not be conformed to this world, but be transformed by the renewing of your mind, that you may prove what is that good and acceptable and perfect will of God" (Romans 12:2).

How will you begin to renew your mind?
How can you discover God's perfect will for your life?

Read 2 Timothy 3:14-17; to find the answers to the above questions.

DAY 4
WHITEWASHED TOMBS

*"For the grace of God that brings salvation
has appeared to all men, teaching us that,
denying ungodliness and worldly lusts we should live soberly,
righteously and godly in this present age,
looking for the blessed hope and glorious appearing
of our great God and Savior, Jesus Christ,
who gave Himself for us. That He might redeem us from every
lawless deed and purify for Himself
His own special people zealous for good works."*
-Reminder from Apostle Paul in Titus 2:11-14

I should have been living a different life, but I also should have been showing grace. We forget it is His grace that is teaching us, redeeming us, and purifying us that enables us to do good works.

I began to take credit for what God was doing in me and through me, though outwardly I was giving Him the glory. This is like the Pharisees Jesus criticized in Matthew 23:27, outwardly conforming but inwardly full of death and decay.

Read Matthew 23:27.

What did Jesus call people who appear to outwardly conform yet inwardly are unchanged by His grace?

Have you been like me and taking credit for what God is doing in and through you?

What is Jesus showing you needs to be changed that you can begin to exemplify His grace to those within your sphere of influence every day?

Day 5
Grow in Grace and Knowledge

*You therefore, beloved, since you know this beforehand, beware lest you also
fall from your own steadfastness,
being led away with the error of the wicked;
but grow in the grace and knowledge
of our Lord and Savior Jesus Christ.*
-2 Peter 3:17-18

I subconsciously intellectualized that I was changing me by changing my habits, my hang outs, and my friends. I did need to separate myself from former friends and previous hang outs or I would have been dragged back into their culture and lifestyle. However, instead of growing in grace and getting stronger so I could go back and confront the culture I came from in love, I just withdrew.

When I did finally go back, I tried shoving the Bible down the throats of friends and unsaved family members which pushed them away from Christ. I had a lot of zeal and head knowledge, but it was not tempered with grace.

Dr. Towns has said, "If Satan can't blind you, he will then attack you in other realms. Sometimes if he can't hold you back from knowing God's will, he will make a fanatic out of you and you will run past the will of God."[1] **This is exactly what happened to me; I got saved, took off like a rocket, and got blindsided by the Devil.**

Where have you been blindsided by the devil because you have not grown in both grace and knowledge?
What is God showing has need of change in your life?

---

[1] Elmer L. Towns is Vice President and Dean of the School of Religion at Liberty University, which he co-founded in 1971 with Jerry Falwell. His books include *Fasting for Spiritual Breakthrough* and *How to Pray When You Don't Know What to Say*.

DAY 6
SELF-RIGHTEOUSNESS

*For I say to you, that unless **your righteousness** exceeds the **righteousness** of the scribes and Pharisees, you will by no means enter the kingdom of heaven.*
-Jesus in Matthew 5:20

This was a progression for me. No one wakes up one morning and says I want to be a drunk, an addict or a legalist living an empty futile life. It is an insidious progressive disease.

First, I was doing the right things because they were right. Then I was doing the right things for the right reasons. Then I was doing the right things because I was supposed to. Then I was doing the right things for others. Finally, I was doing the right things for myself, for my glory, which is **self-righteousness.**

This is as far down into that horrible pit of miry clay that a religious person can go. It is where the alcoholic and addict end up when they hit bottom. This is right where I ended up, quoting scripture as I went as any good self-righteous legalist would do.

Then I read what Jesus said in Matthew 5:20 and it shook me to my core! I had become a legalistic, hypocritical, self-righteous pharisaical

Christian that had lots of knowledge of the scriptures, but not the infilling of His grace to show His love to others.

Read Matthew 23:23-26.
Why does Jesus call the Pharisees hypocrites?
How would you define self-righteousness?
Is this something God is showing you is a problem in your life as well?
How will studying God's grace help you avoid becoming a legalistic, hypocritical, pharisaical Christian?

Day 7
Balance Between Faith and Works

Who is wise and understanding among you?
Let him show by good conduct
that his works are done in the meekness of wisdom.
But the wisdom that is from above is first pure,
then peaceable, gentle, willing to yield, full of mercy and good fruits,
without partiality and without hypocrisy.
-James 3:13 and 17

Colossians 3:23 says, "And whatever you do, do it heartily, as to the Lord and not to men." In Exodus 14:13 Moses says, "Do not be afraid. Stand still and see the salvation of the Lord, which He will accomplish for you today....The Lord will fight for you and you shall hold your peace." These verses express the need to have **a balance between faith and works.** I found myself out of balance.

Without realizing it, my perfectionism, strong will, and desire to please Christ pushed me heavily toward works and legalism. I went to bed tired, woke up tired, and was tired all day. I found myself grumbling and complaining and no matter how good my life was, I wished for something better.

Life was like a merry-go-round that never stopped. Then I read Psalm 46:10, "Be still and know that I am God." It dawned on me that when I stopped and was still before the Lord, the merry-go-round stopped. The longer and more frequently I stopped, the stronger my faith and the more excellent my works became as they were empowered by His Spirit.

I gradually moved out of my strength to His strength, from perfectionism to excellence, and from commitment to surrender.

Is your life like a merry-go-round?

Stop and spend time with the Lord, seek His wisdom, and learn to balance your works with faith and grace.

Week Two
Finally Free

Stand fast therefore in the Liberty by which
Christ has made us free and
do not be entangled again with a yoke of bondage.
-Galatians 5:1

When Jesus cried, "It is finished" in John 19:30, He meant we were free from the punishment, the power, and eventually the presence of sin in our lives. So, why is it so many Christians are entangled in yokes of bondage today? There are many reasons, one of which may be that addictions lead to sin. I will not even begin to attempt an exhaustive explanation, I will just share my own testimony and the insight God has given me to help others walk in freedom from addictions and sin.

When I first accepted Christ as my Savior on April 15, 1987, and knew I was born again, I was immediately freed from the compulsion of three main addictions: alcohol, drugs, and pornography.

Because I had been so miraculously delivered from three extremely powerful addictions, I did not grasp the fact that part of my new life was my responsibility. I did not realize the things I had opened myself up to in my past made me susceptible to addictions of all kinds. I just thought I could pray and read the Bible more and I would not be plagued with my past and other addictions.

However, I was to learn there was more to this new life in Christ than just sitting around and letting Christ do everything for me. Being a new creation in Christ means actively choosing to do things His way and in His timing.

> *Therefore, if anyone is in Christ, he is a new creation; old things have passed away; behold, all things become new.* (2 Corinthians 5:17).

Day 1
Sowing and Reaping

Do not be deceived, God is not mocked;
for whatever a man sows, that will he also reap.
he who sows to his flesh will of the flesh reap corruption, he who sows to the
spirit will of the spirit reap life everlasting.
-Galatians 6:7-8

I had been exposed to a lot of Christianity as a child and could even quote John 3:16. However, like a lot of Americans I did not really believe Satan was real or that there really were consequences to sin. So, I dabbled in things like secular rock music, television, and movies with all their brain washing techniques that Satan uses to introduce us to pornography, alcohol, and drugs.

The corporate world spends millions of dollars for a thirty second commercial during the super bowl because they know that is all it takes to plant a thought and trigger an impulse action.

God has established certain laws, like gravity, that if violated can be fatal or crippling. Like-wise violating His moral laws can be fatal or crippling as well. God established certain rules, safeguards or guidelines for our good so we would not be hurt or hurt others, but all too often we choose to go outside His protection to our own destruction.

"For my thoughts are not your thoughts, nor are your ways My ways," says the Lord (Isaiah 55:8). God has not kept His ways a secret from us. He has given us His written Word to learn how to start thinking and doing things His way.

Read the instructions Jesus gives us in Matthew 6:33.

What does Jesus say our priorities should be? Why?

What changes do you need to make in your life to follow Jesus' instructions?

What did He promise you if you do this?

Day 2
Use the Whole Armor of God

*Put on the whole armor of God, that you may be able
to stand against the wiles of the devil.*
-Ephesians 6:11

Christians are not supposed to be ignorant of Satan's devices, but many have been slowly blinded by letting a little sin into our lives and Satan is taking full advantage of it. "Lest Satan should take advantage of us; for we are not ignorant of his devises" (2 Corinthians 2:11).

Dr. Towns says, "A look at this battle dress tells us that defeating Satan takes the total resources of the total person against an enemy who will bring his total evil plan against us. There is not one inclusive method Christians can use to defeat the devil, such as quoting the Bible. Although the Bible is imperative, it is not the only weapon needed in warfare."

Read Ephesians 6:10-18 and seek to understand each piece of the armor of God so that you can stand against the wiles of the devil.

Verse 12 says our struggle is against: _____

*Verse 14 says we need the belt of_____ in order to _____
_____*

Why is this so important? (See John 8:32) _____

Define righteousness: _____

Verse 16 says we also need the _____

Why? _____

What does the helmet in verse 17 protect? _____

*What are we to use as a weapon and where do we sharpen it?
_____*

*What is another weapon we have (see verse 18)?
_____*

*What is the warning at the end of this verse?
_____*

Day 3
Being Transformed

But we all, with unveiled face,
beholding as in a mirror the glory of the Lord,
are being transformed into the same image.
-2 Corinthian 3:18

Intellectually I knew about sanctification. I knew positionally I was perfect in Christ the moment I believed, but I did not quite get that it was an ongoing continual process.

For me, the process started when my wife left me for another man and I fell into sexual addiction. Though I returned to the Lord, I kept running into that same old feeling time and felt I just could not successfully live the Christian lifestyle.

Then one morning I told the Lord, "I quit, I cannot live the Christian life." **At that moment it was almost as if I heard the Lord say, "Good! Now My Son can live His life through you."** At that moment, a verse I had previously memorized popped into my head, "I have been crucified with Christ; it is no longer I who live, but Christ lives in me; and the life which I now live in the flesh I live by faith in the Son of God, who loved me and gave Himself for me. I do not *set aside* the grace of

God; for if righteousness comes through the law, then Christ died in vain" (Galatians 2:20-21).

There is only one process of transformation that works and that is Christ in us. He transforms us from the inside out.

Read Matthew 15:8-11.
What did Jesus say makes a person defiled or unclean?
Why do you think He said that?
What kind of "talk" comes out of your mouth?
Do your words prove Christ lives in you?

Day 4
Surrender Brings True Freedom

"He who loves father or mother more than Me is not worthy of Me; and he who loves son daughter more than me in not worthy of Me. He who has found his life shall lose it, and he who has lost his life for my sake will find it."
-Jesus in Matthew 10:37-39 (NASB)

The grace of God that I had laid aside was beginning to open up to me in every area of worship. My daily walk, my journaling, doing my daily devotions, my musical tastes expanded immensely, and I desired to give beyond the ten percent tithe required. The desire deep inside my soul woke up and I recognized that God was stirring something inside of me that only a preacher can really understand.

I tried satisfying it by being a substitute teacher for three different adult Sunday school classes, but it only wet my appetite for more. Soon I was talking with my pastor about my desire. We began praying about it together once a week. Then on April 10, 2003, as I was driving between clinics, I felt the presence of God so strong I expected to see Jesus sitting in the passenger seat.

The Lord began speaking to me, though it was not audibly, I knew His voice. The argument lasted about thirty minutes with the Lord calling me to surrender all and go to Bible College and me telling God I could not because I was divorced, had fallen into immorality more than once, I was a single parent, I did not have any money. For every argument I threw out His answer was, "Who is God, Me or you?" I surrendered.

Read Job 38-41 where God speaks to this man and basically asked him the same thing He asked me.

Read Job's reply in Job 42:1-6.

Will you surrender your plans and ideas to God today and allow Him to bring you true freedom in your life?

Day 5
Obedience Brings Freedom

Therefore, prepare your minds for action,
keep sober in spirit, fix your hope completely on the grace
to be brought to you at the revelation of Jesus Christ.
As obedient children, do not be conformed
to the former lusts which were yours in your ignorance.
-1 Peter 1:13-14 (NASB)

As soon as I surrendered, the Lord said, "I want you to go to the Baptist College of Florida." I told the Lord I had very little faith but if He opened the doors I would go. He said, "I want you to call the school today." I argued I could not use my employer's time hoping to buy myself some more time, but the Lord did not let up. So, I promised I would call the school as soon as I got home from work knowing full well the school would be closed by then just to get the Holy Spirit off my back.

Work got extremely busy, I got home late and almost forgot my promise, but the Holy Spirit prompted me so I obediently called. I was completely shocked when someone answered the phone and it was the one lady in charge of sending out admission packets. She told me, after I arrived at the school that she had never been in the office after hours in eighteen years and just happened to stop by that night because her daughter was at a cheerleading event nearby.

Never underestimate the power of God to work out all things according to His purpose (Ephesians 1:11).

Read Ephesians 1:10.
What does this say God created you for?
Do you think He wants you complete your assignment?
Do you think He can and will do whatever is necessary for you to succeed at what He has purposed for you to do?
What does He require of you?

Day 6
Doing God's Will Brings Freedom

"With men it is impossible, but not with God; for with God all things are possible.... Assuredly, I say to you, there is no one who has left house or brothers or sisters or father or mother or wife or children or lands, for My sake and the gospel's, who shall not receive a hundredfold now in this time...and in the age to come, eternal life.
-**Jesus in Mark 10:27, 29-30**

Miracle after miracle ensued. Though I was divorced and had a misdemeanor assault charge from a fight with my ex-wife's boyfriend while we were still married, I was accepted. I found an apartment open on campus so I could have my children with me. I was able to get extra work and save the money to move by staying in my mother's condominium for a month while she was in Maine.

Even the trip to the school campus was a miracle. My transmission blew 450 miles from the campus and I had to spend $600 to be towed into Graceville. My new next door neighbor lent me his wife's car until I could borrow the money to get my truck fixed. Having arrived without a job I trusted the Lord to provide a job for me. Within three days I had two excellent job offers, both better than the one I had left. Only God can do that.

I was finally feeling free because I was doing God's will and things were going good in spite of the trials.

What do you feel God is asking you to do?
Does it seem impossible to you?
What promise did Jesus make in Mark 10:29-30?
Does this promise apply to you?
Will you step out in faith today and do what He is calling you to do even it seems impossible to you?

Day 7
Knowing God Is in Control Brings Freedom

"These things I have spoken to you, that in Me you may have peace. In the world you will have tribulation; but be of good cheer, I have overcome the world."
-Jesus in John 16:33

In August of 2003, I was preparing for my children's return after they spent the summer in Maine with their mother when they notified me that they wanted to try to stay with her for a year. I was devastated, but I turned to the Lord because I was finally free and knew He was in control even though I did not understand. It was a rough start back to college, but I stayed close to the Lord, His word, and His people. I was far from my home with no family, new friends, and a new job. I felt my old addictions pulling at me so I opened up to my next neighbor and his wife to be in prayer for me and to hold me accountable. I also sought the Lord to open up a church for me.

One day my neighbor came over all excited because a church had asked him to recommend someone as a candidate to be their interim Pastor and he told him about me. When they asked him if I was divorced and he told them I was, the Deacon responded, "Good, the best pastor we ever had was a divorced man who went on to be an Evangelist." I began to preach that next Sunday. A day later, a Deacon from another church called me and asked if I would preach at their church. I agreed to preach and asked how he heard about me and he said, "Mr. Hogg's recommended you." I did not know a Mr. Hogg's and never found out who he was, but the next Sunday I was preaching at that church as well.

How does knowing Jesus has overcome the world help you face any tribulations you may encounter doing what God has called you to do?

Week Three
Delight, Commit, and Trust

***Delight** yourself also in the* Lord,
and He shall give you the desires of your heart.
***Commit** your way to the* Lord, ***trust** also in Him,*
and He shall bring it to pass.
-Psalm 37:4-5 (emphasis added)

For the next month I preached every Sunday alternating churches, while going to school and working part-time, but I missed the very point the Lord was trying to make by moving me and taking my children from me. He wanted me to draw all my needs from Him; not Him plus my children, plus my friends, or plus a church. Since I am such a slow learner and the Lord is ever gracious, I continued. Then each church asked me to be their interim pastor. I chose the one that had asked me first and that was where I felt the Lord was leading me.

All of this was happening as I stepped into my new found freedom as a believer. I felt I was finally experiencing the abundant life. Yet, I was still missing the one main point God was trying to get across to me. I believed Psalm 37:4-5, but I did not fully understand all that it meant I was supposed to do. I did not understand my part in the formula.

The Lord, in His infinite wisdom, allowed me to grow as I was for a while. Then on the first day of Thanksgiving break during my morning devotions, the Lord said, "I want you go to Lynchburg and attend Liberty University." The Lord supernaturally opened all the doors for me to go, so I moved again on January 4, 2004.

Delight, commit, and trust were my part of the formula so that God could then give me the desires of my heart. You see, the desires of my heart had to line up with God's plan and purpose for my life in order for Him to bring it to pass in my life.

Day 1
Trust God with All Your Heart

*Trust in the Lord with **all** your heart, and lean not on your own understanding; in **all** your ways acknowledge Him, and He shall direct your paths.*
-Proverbs 3:5-6 (emphasis added)

I settled in my new apartment, got the paperwork done to attend Liberty University for January 2004, and proceeded to get oriented to my new job. I unintentionally made a mistake filling out my job application and did not properly identify a previous misdemeanor. Since I did not mislead them on purpose, I was surprised when I lost the job with its relocation allowance before I finished two weeks of employment.

I knew I was in God's will so I trusted Him and began seeking other employment. My savings were spent, I was living on Ramen noodles, and another month's rent was coming due. I certainly did not understand what God was doing, but I remembered Proverbs 3:5-6. I reminded the Lord He brought me here so He had to provide for me.

I was about to learn what it meant to trust the Lord with all my heart and not rely on my own understanding. When God says all, He means ALL!

Within days I was offered a job doing home physical therapy with a flexible schedule that allowed me to work around my full time class schedule and make more money that I ever had before. Only God can do that and only when I learned to totally trust and rely only on Him!

*What does it mean to trust the Lord with **all** your heart?*
*What does it mean to acknowledge God in **all** your ways?*
*When God says **all** what does He mean?*
Do you see any "exception" clauses in His promise?

Day 2
The Paul and Silas Solution

And when they had laid many stripes on them, they threw them into prison, commanding the jailer to keep them securely. Having received such a charge, he put them into the inner prison and fastened their feet in the stocks. But at midnight Paul and Silas were praying and singing hymns to God, and the prisoners were listening to them.

-Acts 16:23-25

I was learning the Paul and Silas solution to trials. When you get to the dead end and when you are at the end of your rope, Paul and Silas demonstrated for us that is the time to start praising God. What did they know that many Christians have not yet discovered? When you rely on and trust in God, if your circumstances do not change, but your attitude does then God will use your testimony to help you and others.

I believe what they were showing is us is how to delight ourselves in the Lord no matter what the circumstances in our lives.

I began to realize I needed this time alone with God to deepen my relationship with Him so I could become all that He had called me to be.

School was going good and my job was going well. I was starting to make friends at church and had near daily phone contact with my children.

Though they were still in Maine, with each call I sensed their restlessness was growing. I chose to praise God for all that He had done for me and all that He was doing in my life and all those He brought me into contact with on a regular basis.

Study the following verses from the Psalms and begin to delight in the Lord, in His Word, and in His way.

Record in your journal what God reveals to you from each one. Praise Him today for His presence in your life.

Psalm 1:2, 37:4, 40:8, 112:1, 119:24, 119:143.

Day 3
Refreshing From His Presence

Repent therefore and be converted,
that your sins may be blotted out,
so that times of refreshing may come
from the presence of the Lord,
and that He may send Jesus Christ,
who was preached to you before.
-Acts 3:19-20

Not only was the knowledge I had previously learned in my early Christian life coming back to me, but I was also growing in grace in a new and living way. Yet there was that gnawing in the back of my mind that not all was firing on all cylinders. I was growing in grace and knowledge while finally becoming free from all my bondages (or so I thought) yet there was an apprehension in my soul.

As I spent more and more time in His presence, I realized I could show others God's love and grace without accepting their behavior. I learned to accept those who had fallen regardless of where they were in their recovery just as God had accepted me.

The Lord gave me this revelation several years ago as I was sharing my testimony with a friend and it has continued to make sense to me as one fallen and come back to Him.

Like a beautiful tapestry, sometimes it is hard to tell if we are walking away from a pattern of behavior or walking toward a pattern of behavior because we are still too close to the pattern.

Only by spending time in God's presence can we begin to see things from His perspective.

Set aside time today to spend in the presence of your loving heavenly Father. Record your thoughts in your journal.

Day 4
Commit Your Way to Him

I solemnly charge you in the presence of God and of Christ Jesus, who is to judge the living and the dead, and by His appearing and His kingdom: preach the word; be ready in season and out of season; reprove, rebuke, exhort, with great patience and instruction. For the time will come when they will not endure sound doctrine; but wanting to have their ears tickled, they will accumulate for themselves teachers in accordance to their own desires, and will turn away their ears from the truth and will turn aside to myths. But you, be sober in all things, endure hardship, do the work of an evangelist, fulfill your ministry.
-Apostle Paul to his disciple in 2 Timothy 4:1-5 (NASB)

I have always known I was called as a preacher to herald and proclaim with practical application what I have learned through study and experience in my own life. Every spiritual test I have taken has also shown me I have the gift of exhortation (empathy, encouragement and support) and also of discernment (distinguishing between truth and error, pure and impure motives).

As I sought to fulfill the ministry God has given me and use the gifts He has placed within me, I read Proverbs 16:3 which says, "Commit your works to the Lord, and your thoughts will be established." Colossians 3:23-24 gave me further sound advice, "Whatever you do, do your work heartily, as for the Lord rather than for men.... It is the Lord Christ whom you serve" (NASB).

Read Joshua 24:15 and *choose for yourself today whom you will serve.*

Day 5
Victory in Jesus

How can a young man keep his way pure?
By keeping it according to Your word.
-Psalm 119:9 (NASB)

I was seeking to stay balanced and sensitive to God while working toward fulfilling my ministry, using my gifts, and actively seeking Him. The Lord loves me enough to continue to show me my selfishness, my self-centeredness, the lust that is in me, the impurity, the pride, and self-sufficiency. As I see it, repent, and cry out for His cleansing, I am healed. As I surrender it all to Christ, confess my sins, and lay my addictions at the foot of the Cross, I realize the power of every sin and addiction is broken, but I need to leave it at the cross where the victory was won for me.

Sin and addiction are both the absence of God from some area of my life, so He helps me see where I have shut Him out and then the power of that sin or addiction is broken. Psalm 37:4-5, 73:26, and Matthew 6:33 help me keep Christ first. Though we stumble we shall not be utterly cast down, for the Lord upholds us with his hand (Psalm 37:24).

What has the Lord been showing you needs to be confessed and brought to the foot of the cross?
Will you repent and leave it at the cross with Jesus?

Read Psalm 37:4-5, 24 and 73:26. Also read Matthew 6:33.
How have these verses encouraged you today?
Think on them as you go through your day today.

Record in your journal all that He is revealing to you today.
Thank Him that your victory is available through your trust and commitment to Him.

Day 6
Accountability Is a Must!

*Therefore, confess your sins to one another,
and pray for one another so that you may be healed.
The effective prayer of a righteous man
can accomplish much.*
-James 5:16 (NASB)

James 5:16 tells us to confess our faults one to another that we may healed. There are a few close accountability partners I feel safe being absolutely transparent with that I can ask to pray with me when I need healing or strength to stay on track.

Hebrews 10:24-25 tells us, "Let us consider one another in order to stir up love and good works, not forsaking the assembling of ourselves together." There are to be no lone ranger Christians. The Apostle Paul reminds us in 1 Corinthians 12:12 and 27, "For even as the body is one and *yet* has many members, and all the members of the body, though they are many, are one body, so also is Christ. Now you are Christ's body, and individually members of it" (NASB).

Read 1 Corinthians 12:12-27.

Why is it important to have accountability?
Who are your accountability partners?
If you do not have someone you can trust, ask the Lord to lead you to the right person.
Why is it important to encourage one another?
Why is it important to work together with other members of the Body of Christ?
Ask the Lord to show you how to become a more active member of His Body.
Journal all that the Lord reveals to you today.

Day 7
What if You Miss the Mark?

For I am confident of this very thing,
that He who began a good work in you will perfect it
until the day of Christ Jesus.
-Philippians 1:6

God's grace and mercy extend to us even when we miss the mark. I had to learn that sanctification is a process with perfection being the end result. Though I strive to that end, I know in this life I will make mistakes along the way though I press on toward that mark. If God can restore me for the upward calling in Christ Jesus, then I know He can heal and restore you as well.

I pray the Holy Spirit will use the verses from God's Word throughout this book to bring conviction and repentance in those areas where you may need it and that my testimony will bring comfort and hope in areas where you may be struggling.

Please, do not give up hope. Continue to press on toward the mark God is revealing to you.

Read the stories in the Bible of those who missed the mark and were used mightily by God in spite of their weaknesses. Record your thoughts in your journal.

King David committed adultery and murder, but then God said David was a man after God's heart (see 2 Samuel 11-12, and Acts 13:22).

Peter, a disciple of Jesus, denied Him three times, but then was commission by Jesus to be the leader of the Jerusalem church (see Matthew 26:69-75, John 21:15-23).

Paul persecuted the early Christians before meeting Jesus on the road to Damascus (see Acts 8:1 and 9:1-9).

Though he wrote the majority of the New Testament, God even gave him a thorn in the flesh to keep him from becoming prideful (see 2 Corinthians 12:7).

Week Four
A Call to Sexual Purity

For this is the will of God, your sanctification:
that you should abstain from sexual immorality;
that each of you should abstain from sexual immorality;
that each of you should know how to possess his own vessel in sanctification
and honor, not in passion or lust,
like the Gentiles who do not know God.
(1 Thessalonians 4:3-5)

We have natural God given desires, but all of those desires are to be controlled by His principles and boundaries we are not to cross. However, many feel, as I once did, that these are outdated and that God is just trying to keep us from having fun. On the contrary, God put those boundaries there so He could keep us for true joy with a pure heart and conscience that would not be defiled.

Romans 1:18-32 shows our rebellion against God and what violating His law does to us. God gave me up to my own selfish pleasures for a while because He knew there was no joy in them for me. I knew the pleasures of sin were for a season, but there is a difference between knowing and believing. I know a chair can hold me by looking at it, but I believe a chair can hold me by sitting in it.

I knew sin would take me further than I wanted to go, keep me longer than I wanted to stay, and cost me more than I wanted to pay, but my strong will had to experience this failure first hand.

I can only imagine how hard it was for God, like it was for the father in the Parable of the Prodigal Son, to watch me choose to go my own way.

Day 1
The Prodigal Son

And not many days later, the younger son gathered everything together and went on a journey into a distant country, and there he squandered his estate with loose living.
-Luke 15:13 (NASB)

The prodigal son in Luke 15:11-24 is the classic example of my life after I had received Christ. Once I had accepted Christ as my Savior and turned from my sin, I was made a child of God. Then I chose to turn from His grace like the prodigal son. It was not until I hit bottom in my fallen state that I came to myself and realized I was not worthy to be called one of His sons (Luke 15:17-20).

I knew what I was doing was wrong initially, but the further into sin I went the less discernment I had left to see or make right choices. It was not so much God giving up on me because His chastisement was always present. I was getting so spiritually blind that I could no longer see just how deep the pit I was digging for myself was becoming.

In fact, the worse my spiritual eyesight became, the further into sin I went thinking everything was justifiable. I was only acting like everyone else around me. It was not pornography or sexual immorality that held me there, but the desire for a companion, a help-mate, a new wife.

Read the entire Parable of the Prodigal Son in Luke 15:11-24.

Have you ever gotten impatient waiting for God to answer your prayer?

Did you try and take things into your own hands?

How did that turn out for you?

What caused the Prodigal Son to come to his senses?

Have you ever felt your choices were justifiable even though you knew they were not what God told you to do?

Day 2
The Horrible Pit of Sin

But among you there must not be even a hint of sexual immorality, or of
any kind of impurity, or of greed,
because these are improper for God's holy people.
-Ephesians 5:3 (NIV)

The climb back up out of that horrible pit of sin was so much harder the second time around. There was no instant deliverance from compulsions; there was no decreasing of the natural desires while I healed and grew. All I could ever think of during this second time of recovery was, "For it would have been better for them not to have known the way of righteousness, than having known it, to turn from the holy commandment delivered to them. But it has happened to them according to the true proverb: 'A dog returns to his own vomit,' and 'a sow, having washed, to her wallowing in the mire'" (2 Peter 2:21-22 NASB).

It was coming back up out of this despair with the mistakes I was making in search of a new wife that forced me to realize I must be completely pure. The only way to finally break the bonds of the addiction to this sin off of my life was to not allow even a hint of sexual immorality in my life.

In order to break the addiction you have to deal with the sin. This is true of any sin, but especially of sexual sin because of its appeal to our most basic need. We are all looking to have that most basic need of being fulfilled with a companion, but when we violate God's law we can become addicted to what we have exposed ourselves to.

* *Why does the Bible say there must not be even a hint of sexual immorality?*
* *If you want to keep an intruder out of your home, what must you do to the doors and windows?*
* *So, what must you do to your mind and your heart?*

Day 3
Prayer and Fasting

"However, this kind does not go out
except by prayer and fasting."
-Matthew 17:21

The brain is just an organ, neither moral nor immoral and when it desires something is when we act. However, I did not realize the choice was mine to make. I can chose to sin or not to sin. I also did not realize the power of a life time habit ingrained inside of me was triggering me biologically.

Dr. Mark R. Laaser, says in his book, *Healing the Wounds of Sexual Addiction*, "Abstinence (for ninety days) reverses the sex addict's core belief that 'Sex in my most important need.'"

When I was in Alcoholics Anonymous, I went to ninety meetings in ninety days, quit hanging around the same places with the same friends, and had absolutely no alcohol. It amazes me that people think you can hold on to a little sin and still overcome an addiction to it. Ninety days of abstinence or fasting is nothing when it comes to saving a marriage or a wrecked life!

The longer I am in recovery and the more people I see struggling, the more I realize that sexual sin takes fasting and fervent prayer to overcome, just like Jesus said.

By the third or fourth month of fasting and prayer, I noticed the pull was diminished almost completely. However, I had to keep practicing all the things I had learned to that point.

* *How much is it worth to you to overcome your addiction?*

* *Would you be willing to invest in a ninety-day fast to attain the victory over your addictive sin?*

Day 4
Take Up Your Cross Daily

"If anyone desires to come after Me, let him deny himself, and take up his cross daily, and follow Me.
For whoever desires to save his life will lose it,
but whoever loses his life for My sake will save it."
-Luke 9:23-24

For me to continue in victory, I realized I must take up my cross daily and follow Jesus. The forty-day fast taught me I could deny my body its natural desire for food without any adverse consequences. In fact, it opened my eyes to deeper spiritual things than ever before. I figured if I could deny myself something as basic as food, I could also deny myself any other form of addictive behavior. Applying that principle gave me more freedom, because in this life and in this culture temptations abound.

I was no longer interested in seeing how close I could get to sin and remain free. I knew I had found the way to freedom that even the world is looking for.

The closer I stay to Christ and the more I desire to be like Him, the easier it gets. This also fills me with a realistic confidence that with Him, I can conquer my own addiction and help others conquer theirs as well.

* *What is the way to freedom talked about here?*
* *How can you apply this principle to your own life?*
* *Do you have the kind of confidence you need to conquer your addictive behavior?*
* *How can you use what you have learned to help others conquer their addictive behavior?*
* *Remember to record your thoughts in your journal.*

Day 5
Refuse the Victim Mentality

Being confident of this very thing,
that He who has begun a good work in you
will complete it until the day of Jesus Christ.
-Philippians 1:6

God has done His part in saving me and keeping me. My part is to surrender my will and cooperate with Him. It does not matter what fiery trials come my way because my circumstances do not dictate my behavior anymore. Satan would love to have me spend all my energy fighting trivial issues so I do not focus on the root of the problem, which is me.

Like so many others in this world, I was victimized at a young age, but I refuse to stay in that victim mentality. I used to think if only I had not been raped as a child, if only I had not been exposed to pornography, if only my childhood had been more guarded by my parents, and the list went on and on and on.

Then it dawned on me, I have everything I will ever need in Christ to overcome the past and continue in victory into the future.

My past victories and past defeats are behind me (Philippians 3:13-14). I can learn from them, but God, my Father, is greater than all those things and He cares for me.

Read Philippians 3:13-14.

* *What are we supposed to forget about?*
* *What are we supposed to do instead?*
* *What is our goal supposed to be?*
* *Why do you think this is so important?*
* *Who are we supposed to put our confidence in?*
* *Why?*

Day 6
Trust God to Fulfill Every Need

And my God will meet all your needs
according to the riches of his glory in Christ Jesus.
-Philippians 4:19 NIV

I began to trust God to fulfill me in every way, even in my unmet needs. I began to truly believe all sin, especially addictions, are a result of not allowing Christ in some area of my life. I began to look to see if there was some hidden desire that I had not opened up to Him so He could fulfill it. The consequences of not trusting Him to fulfill that need would eventually lead me away from Him toward addiction.

What I discovered was I had a need for companionship that was not even necessarily connected to a sexual need. I was trying to fulfill that need on my own. The end result was I realized I could trust God to meet my need for companionship even as a single parent among all the temptations that abound all around me.

In fact, many preachers have said marriage is a foretaste of the delight we will have in Heaven. It is a picture of the level of relationship we will have with Christ as His bride. It was putting this altogether that helped me realize I could have that type of close relationship with Christ now and that was what He wanted of me all along.

It finally dawned on me that God knows what we need and He is willing and able to fulfill that need when we come to Him trusting He knows what is best for us.

* *Are there needs in your life you have never thought to ask God to fulfill for you?*
* *Why not express that need to Him right now and tell Him you will trust He will give you exactly what you need to bring fulfillment in your life.*
* *Remember to record in your journal all that you learn.*

Day 7
The Act of Repentance

If we confess our sins,
He is faithful and just to forgive us our sins
and to cleanse us from all unrighteousness.
-1 John 1:9

The only way to get back right with God is repentance. According to Steve Gallagher, "To grasp true repentance, one must comprehend the nature of sin. A person sins whenever he willfully acts upon a fleshy impulse to do something that has been forbidden by God. In other words, he rejects God's will in favor of his own. So, any attempt to find freedom from habitual sin while remaining in self-will is futile. The act of repentance involves a confession that one's behavior and a submission of God's will."[2]

---

[2] The first and best book I read on as a person coming out of sexual addiction was, *At The Altar OF Sexual Idolatry* by Steve Gallagher because of its biblical content. It is a powerful and comprehensive examination of a person trapped in the bondage of sexual sin. His latest book is just as powerful because he has a compassionate heart and dedication to help men overcome sexual sin through the application of the Bible. For other great references, go to the Appendix section at the end of this book.

Submission to God means admitting we have sinned, without excuses or blame, and asking for His forgiveness. When we do, He not only cleanses us of all unrighteousness, He then takes our mess and makes it a powerful message to bring others to Him as well.

Though the scars I received are many, I know God can take what the devil meant for evil and turn it into good so that not one of my wounds are wasted.

*Will you allow God to turn your mess into a powerful message of forgiveness and love?

Week Five
Resisting Temptation

Let no one say when he is tempted, "I am tempted of God; for God cannot be tempted by evil, nor does He himself tempt anyone. But, each one is tempted when he is drawn away by his own desired and enticed. Then, when desire had conceived, it gives birth to sin; and sin, when it is full grown, brings forth death."
–James 1:13-14 NKJV

In spite, of all my failures the Lord has been gracious to allow me to get back up and continue on in the fight. However, I did not understand, as the above verse clearly points out, **all people are tempted**.

One of the first things I learned in this progressive growth toward victory was I had an enemy within. There was a traitor in the camp that I had to deal with, but I did not have the power to handle. **This traitor was my old nature.**

"The heart is deceitful above all things, and desperately wicked; who can know it? I, the Lord, search the heart; I test the mind, even to give every man according to his ways, according to the fruit of his doings" (Jeremiah 17:9 NKJV).

I was truly beginning to see just how wicked my heart was by comparing myself to God's Word and to His ideal as He revealed Himself in the person of His Son, Jesus Christ. So I asked the Lord, "Search me O God, and know my heart; Try me, and know my anxieties; And see if there is any wicked way in me and , lead me in the way everlasting" (Psalm 139:23-24). The Lord began to show me where there was still sin in my life, whether it was things I was doing that I should not be doing (sins of commission) or things that I was not doing that I should be doing (sins of omission). I was also starting to realize attitudes and words were as bad as actions, but had different consequences and it was grieving me in my spirit.

Day 1
Dealing with Pride

*For from within, out of the heart of men,
proceed evil thoughts, adulteries, fornications, murders, thefts, covetousness,
wickedness, deceit, lewdness,
an evil eye, blasphemy, pride, foolishness.
All these evil things come from within and defile a man.*
– Mark 7:20-23

The closer I drew to Christ the more I could see these things in me. Pride has always been a huge stumbling block for me. I had to learn that even my service to Him was "not by might nor by power, but by His Spirit" (Zechariah 4:6). All the good I was doing was enabled by His unseen hand (Philippians 2:13).

It was the Lord who gave me strength and took away my weakness. It was the Lord who gave me soundness of mind and took away my insanity. **It was who the Lord gave me healing and took away my addictions, all for His glory!**

The Lord said to me, "'So here's what I want you to do, take your everyday, ordinary life—your sleeping, eating, going-to-work, and walking-around life—and place it before Me as an offering.' Embracing what

God does for you is the best thing you can do for Him. Don't become so well-adjusted to your culture that you fit into it without even thinking. Instead, fix your attention on God. You'll be changed from the inside out. Readily recognize what He wants from you, and quickly respond to it. Unlike the culture around you, always dragging you down to its level of immaturity, God brings the best out of you, develops well-formed maturity in you" (Romans 12:1-2 MSG).

List the steps of surrender and the benefits of offering everything in your life to Him. Use it as your to do list today and every day to begin to overcome the traitor within you.

Day 2
Dealing with Deception

*But I am afraid that just as Eve was deceived
by the serpent's cunning, your minds may somehow
be led astray from your sincere and pure devotion to Christ.*
-2 Corinthians 11:3

Satan is master deceiver. If he can't get to you one way him will just come around to a different door of the same house. He is relentless. He may come as a roaring lion (1 Peter 5:8) or as an angel of light (2 Corinthians 11:14). We are never to let our guard down.

A temptation takes but a second to turn into a sin, and once you sin, Satan has his hooks in you and you will pay the consequences. No person has and no person will ever get away with a single sin. "Some men's sins are clearly evident, preceding them to judgment, but those of some men follow after" (1 Timothy 5:24), but you can be sure your sin will find you out (Numbers 32:23).

1 Corinthians 5:6-8 clarified a lot of areas of deception for me. "Do you not know that a little leavens the whole lump? Therefore purge out the old leaven, that you may be a new lump, since you truly are unleavened. For indeed Christ, our Passover was sacrificed for us. Therefore let

us keep the feast, not with old leaven *(for me this was a works based system of thoughts and deeds of my flesh)*, nor with the leaven of malice and wickedness *(for me this was the sinful thoughts and deeds of my flesh)*, but with the unleavened bread of sincerity and truth *(for me this was focusing solely on Christ in worship)*" (1 Corinthians 5:6-8).

* *Go back to 1 Corinthians 5:6-8 and insert your own "old leaven" and your own "malice and wickedness."*

* *Then ask God to show you what your "unleavened bread of sincerity and truth" are to be to overcome the Satan's deception in your life.*

Day 3
Take My Yoke upon You

"Take My yoke upon you and learn from Me,
for I am gentle and humble in heart,
and YOU WILL FIND REST FOR YOUR SOULS.
For My yoke is easy and My burden is light."
-Matthew 11:29-30 (NASB)

Having God search my heart was humbling, but it was much easier than being humiliated by sin. My heart was the opposite of submission, glorying self is not good. I had begun to learn it was better to be humble then humiliated and better to be transparent than exposed so God could heal me, fill me, and use me.

Old things were now truly passing away and all things were becoming new, but it came as a process as I grew and renewed my mind by a deep intimate knowledge of who Christ truly is (Colossians 3:9-10). The Lord began showing me boundaries that many would consider old-fashioned, but I knew were designed for my good.

I made a vow not to date for a year which enabled me to look and treat women with no ulterior motives. I knew I was complete in Christ, "And you are complete in Him, who is the head of all principality and power" (Colossians 2:10).

I continued to immediately capture every thought that was drifting after my own fleshly desires. The more I did it, the faster and easier it became. All these techniques strengthened by the Holy Spirit were part of the sacrifices the Lord was calling me to; the yoke He was asking me to bear. I had labored and had been heavily burdened for years on my own without rest. **I finally gave up the yoke of bondage to take His yoke and found true rest for my soul.**

* *Are you heavily burdened trying to resist temptation?*
* *What is Jesus telling you to do to find true rest for your soul? Why not start today?*

DAY 4
DON'T LET YOUR GUARD DOWN

Do not love the world or the things in world.
If anyone loves the world, the love of the Father is not in him. For all this is the world-the lust of the flesh, the lust of the eyes, and the pride of life-is not of the Father but is of the world. And the world is passing away, and the lust of it;
but him who does the will of God abides forever.
-1 John 2:15-17

How did I, as a believer, get to such a despicable place? I never asked to have multiple addictions nor did I purposely seek to backslide, but I let my guard down. I let my guard down in just a few areas and the enemy came in like a flood. Instead of dealing with the things I could see were wrong, I let them lay there and fester until the rottenness of decay blinded me to everything except what I wanted.

I began putting my will above God's will, resurrecting one old idol after another. My flesh craved more and more so I rose up new idols. I had become my own god because I knew what I needed when I needed it. The desire did not seem to matter, *the lust of the flesh, the lust of the eyes, and the pride of life;* it was like changing hats. It was pornography, relationships, food addictions, alcohol, recognition, attention, being well-liked, perfectionism, excelling at my job, and so on. Whenever that particular idol lost its allure, it went into the closet and another came out and took its place.

Because I let my guard in one or two little areas and stopped exercising myself to godliness I grew weak.

* *Are there areas in your life where you have let your guard down?*
* *Have "idols" begun to fill your life instead of God?*
* *What has God shown you that needs to be destroyed and removed from your life?*

Day 5
Exercise Godliness

But reject profane and old wives' fables, and exercise yourself toward godliness. For bodily exercise profits a little, but godliness is profitable for all things, having the promise of the life that now is and of that which is to come.
-1 Timothy 4:7-8

Just like in the physical realm, when I stopped exercising and eating right I became an undisciplined glutton. "But Israel soon became fat and unruly; the people grew heavy, plump, and stuffed! Then they abandoned the God who had made them; they made light of the Rock of their salvation" (Deuteronomy 32:15 NLT). Like the nation of Israel, I had gotten fat spiritually and thought I no longer needed God. Without God in my life, I created a vacuum that I began to try to fill with all these other things.

Spiritually I was sick and getting sicker by the day, and it began showing up physically.

I gained a lot of weight, I lost hair due to stress and improper nutrition, my memory was affected, and I began to age faster. Most all I was tired all the time. I think it was the fatigue that really got to me.

So, I cried out to God asking Him to empower me by His Holy Spirit and give me an old fashioned Holy Ghost revival to my soul.

Have you noticed any physical changes in your life?
Trace these changes back and discover the root cause.
Have you stopped exercising godliness in your life?
Have you become spiritually sick?
Ask God to give you a Holy Spirit revival and empower you to make the changes you need to make starting today.

Day 6
Get an Attitude Adjustment

God, after He spoke long ago to the fathers in the prophets
in many portions and in many ways,
in these last days has spoken to us in His Son,
whom He appointed heir of all things,
through whom also He made the world.
-Hebrews 1:1-2 (NASB)

My attitudes began to change. No longer was I the prideful know-it-all. I realized I could learn from everyone if I kept my heart and mind open to hear. I knew in these last days God was speaking to us in His Son, Jesus Christ. Then, I also began to understand Jesus was speaking to me through various people saved and unsaved.

God was speaking to me all the time; I was just not listening. So I began practicing God's presence in my daily life all the time. As I spent quality time with God, I began to glean more from the scriptures and discern how I was to use what He was teaching me in my day-to-day life.

As my attitude changed and I realized I had to obey *all* of 1 Timothy 5:1-2. Though I might be called to rebuke an older man, I was not to do it harshly, but exhort him and treat him with respect as a father. I was also to treat the younger men as brothers, the older women as mothers, and the younger women as sisters with all purity.

As you go through your day, watch for ways God speaks to through others.
Spend quality time with God and learn to listen for His still small voice speaking to you through the scriptures.
Diligently record all that you learn from your time with God and from those He sends across your path.
Use what you learn to help others grow and learn, too.

Day 7
A Warning

For this reason we must pay much closer attention to what we have heard, so that we do not drift away from it. For if the word spoken through angels proved unalterable, and every transgression and disobedience received a just penalty, how will we escape if we neglect so great a salvation? After it was at the first spoken through the Lord, it was confirmed to us by those who heard, God also testifying with them, both by signs and wonders and by various miracles and by gifts of the Holy Spirit according to His own will.
-Hebrews 2:1-4 (NASB emphasis added)

Even at forty, the youthful lusts were as strong as they were when I was in my twenties. I had to, "Flee also youthful lusts; but pursue righteousness, faith, love, peace, with those who call on the Lord out of a pure heart" (2 Timothy 2:22).

I had been sucked in by the world's system that I had once escaped from and it was draining the life out of me, literally. When I chose to walk away from God, I was unable to resist temptation. However, when I began to once again pay much closer attention to what I had heard and been taught, I began to overcome the temptations all around me, and I grew strong enough to truly help others as well.

I'd had to get to a place where there was nowhere to go but up. I had to acknowledge that only the Lord Jesus Christ could do the work in me and then through me.

I pray this week's devotions showed you how to avoid the pits I fell into and how to deal with temptation in the only real effective way.

* *What did you learn this week that has made a difference in your attitudes and approach to dealing with the temptations all around you?*

* *Make sure you journal what you have learned this week.*

Week Six
Damaged by Divorce

And He answered and said to them, "Have you not read that He who made them as the beginning made them male and female, and said, 'For this reason a man shall leave his father and mother and be joined to his wife, and the two shall become one flesh'? So then, they are no longer two but one flesh. Therefore what God has joined together, let not man separate." They said to Him, "Why then did Moses command to give a certificate of divorce, and to put her away?" He said to them, "Moses, because of the hardness of your hearts permitted you to divorce your wives, but from the beginning it was not so. And I say to you, whoever divorces his wife, except for sexual immorality, and marries another, commits adultery; and whoever marries her who is divorced commits adultery."
-Matthew 19:4-9 NKJV

Damaged by divorce is what I felt I was every time I walked into a church or a Christian fellowship. It did not matter whether it was

Sunday morning, Wednesday night, a church fellowship, or a picnic. It did not matter if it was at someone's home or at a conference retreat. I felt as if I had a big "D" branded on my forehead for all to see I was divorced and that I was damaged goods.

The Bible may say the unpardonable sin is rejecting Christ, but as a divorced person, I felt like I had committed the unpardonable sin by allowing my ex-wife to divorce me. Though I fought the divorce for over five months, would not file for it, and prayed against it, I still felt like I had committed the unpardonable sin.

Day 1
God's Perfect Will

But from the beginning it was not so.
-Matthew 19:8

I began to wonder if I would ever be allowed to use my spiritual gifts of preaching, teaching, and shepherding now that I was divorced. I wondered if I was to be put on the shelf, no longer able to be used of God. Did my past immorality negate my present walk with Christ? Was it that God only gave us one chance with marriage in the church and everything else meant I could not serve Him as I used to?

So I began to study what Jesus said in Matthew 19:4-9. He began this discussion on divorce by explaining God's perfect will to both the Pharisees and the large crowds following Him. Jesus asked them if they had read Genesis 2:24, *"Have you not read that He who made them as the beginning made them male and female, and said, 'For this reason a man shall leave his father and mother and be joined to his wife, and the two shall become one flesh'? So then, they are no longer two but one flesh. Therefore what God has joined together, let not man separate."*

When God instituted marriage in the Garden of Eden by performing the very first wedding ceremony, He intended for the man and the woman to become intimate and remain in that relationship for the rest of their lives.

Later, Jesus said, *"Moses, because of the hardness of your hearts, permitted you to divorce your wives, but from the beginning it was not so.* "Permitted" to me is not God's perfect will.

God allows us to choose to sin, but that is not His will for any believer and neither is divorce.

* *What is God's perfect will for marriage?*
* *What does Malachi 2:16 say about divorce?*

Day 2
The God of Reconciliation

*All this is from God, who reconciled us to himself
through Christ and gave us the ministry of reconciliation:
that God was reconciling the world to himself in Christ,
not counting people's sins against them.
And he has committed to us the message of reconciliation. We are therefore
Christ's ambassadors,
as though God were making his appeal through us.
We implore you on Christ's behalf: Be reconciled to God.*
-2 Corinthians 5:18-20 (NIV)

Our God is the God of reconciliation. He reconciled Himself to sinful mankind through the blood of His Son on the cross. Once we choose to accept God's terms for reconciliation, He makes us His ambassadors to the lost world so they can also be reconciled to God through Jesus Christ.

I believe God understands divorce when there is abuse and a life is in danger. I believe He understands divorce when there is habitual sexual immorality. I also believe divorce is usually a sin because it is not God's will, it is the people who divorce who exert their will over God's. I believe

God hates divorce for the same reason Him hates any sin because of all the pain and harm it causes His children.

Sin is basically disobedience to God's way and His plan. When we miss the mark, we can go to Him, be forgiven, and reconciled through the blood of Jesus Christ. Then we can be used as His ambassadors to the lost.

* As the Apostle Paul said in 2 Corinthians 5:20, *"We implore you on Christ's behalf: Be reconciled to God."*

* *Ask Him to show you how He would use you as His ambassador to the lost.*

Day 3
Remarriage?

"Now to the married I command yet not I but the Lord:
A wife is not to depart from her husband.
But, even if she does depart, let her remain unmarried
or be reconciled to her husband.
And a husband is not to divorce his wife."
-1 Corinthians 7:10-11

I struggled as my wife lived with another man because I had in my heart to obey the Lord. I wanted to see Him get a hold of her heart and for her to choose to come back. However, after two and a half years, she married her boyfriend and I knew I was free to remarry without any doubts. I felt Deuteronomy 24:1-4 actually forbid me to remarry her once she had chosen to marry another man.

When a man takes a wife and marries her, and it happens that she finds no favor in his eyes because he has found some uncleanness in her, and he writes her a certificate of divorce, and sends her out of his house, when she has departed from his house, and goes and becomes another man's wife, if the latter husband detests her and writes her a certificate of divorce, puts it in her hand, and sends her out of his house, or if the latter husband detests dies who took her as his wife, then her former husband who divorced her must not take her back to his wife after she has defiled; for that is an abomination before the Lord, and you shall not bring sin on the land which the Lord your God is giving you as an inheritance. (Deuteronomy 24:1-4)

God's way is always for what is best for us. He loves us and welcomes us back to Him just like the Father in the Parable of the Prodigal Son.

* *Seek His way first and you will see the blessings flow.*
* *Do this by spending time with Him daily.*

Day 4
Dealing with the Scars of Divorce

"You did not choose Me, but I chose you and appointed (ordained) you that you should go and bear fruit, and that your fruit should remain, that whatever you ask the Father in My name Him may give it to you."
-John 15:16

Unfortunately, in this life there is not always repentance or it comes too late and another marriage has taken place. There is bitterness that needs to be dealt with, scars that need to be healed, and acceptance of things beyond your control.

Though the bitterness was fairly easy to take care of because I could see it and sincerely confess it, it did not go away all at once. When it resurfaced, I sensed it and brought it before the Lord and He helped me let it go. It was easier every time to accept His full healing and let go of the bitterness.

However, accepting the consequences of divorce was a huge deal for me and one that stalled my healing for quite a while. I could not get away from my calling as a preacher, teacher, and shepherd though it seemed I was now disqualified from using my God given gifts. At first I felt like I was fighting against the current, but then like everything else in my life, I decided to let God handle it His way.

I prayed and told Him if opened the doors, I would go and do what He had called me to do. In the meantime, I would be a faithful single dad and raise my children honoring God and His Word. That was exactly what He wanted me to do.

* *The best way to be used of God is to make yourself available to His plan, His way, and in His timing.*
* *The only way to tap into His plan is to spend time in His presence daily.*

Day 5
Not Damaged, Not Lacking

Consider it pure joy, my brothers and sisters,
whenever you face trials of many kinds,
because you know that the testing of your faith produces perseverance. Let
perseverance finish its work so that
you may be mature and complete, not lacking anything.
-James 1:2-4 (NIV)

The Lord began undoing the feeling of being damaged goods through His love and acceptance. I simply sought to do what He wanted me to do, when He wanted me to do it, and left the rest up to Him.

I began to realize that with His grace I could overcome anything and face every trial with joy. I just needed to "keep pressing on for that upward call in Christ Jesus" (Philippians 3:14). The more He healed me and the more grace I experienced, the more I cried tears of joy every time I preached or shared my testimony.

It did not matter if I was preaching, teaching or just sharing in a support group, when He poured forth His love, people received me as His ambassador and lives were healed. **That is when there was true joy and fulfilment in my life.**

God can and will repair even what the world considers a life damaged beyond repair. There are many stories in the Bible about "damaged" people God used mightily for His glory. David, the adulterer and murderer; Rahab, the harlot; and Samson, the womanizer to name just a few. Read their stories and realize you are not beyond God's healing hands.

Take time to read the stories of the great "heroes" in the Bible and see how God healed and then used them.
Record what you discover in your journal.

Day 6
Comforted to Comfort

*Praise be to the God and Father of our Lord Jesus Christ, the Father of
compassion and the God of all comfort,
who comforts us in all our troubles,
so that we can comfort those in any trouble
with the comfort we ourselves receive from God.*
-2 Corinthians 1:3-4 (NIV)

God did not heal me for the sake of healing me. He healed me so He could use me to help others. In fact, it was out of my healing that my vision came. I knew I wanted to help others, but I was not sure how. My vision started small, though it quickly grew. I wanted to start an in-patient treatment center for addicts of all sorts to find the healing forgiveness of God's love in Jesus His Son just as I have.

I envisioned a place where those who have been ravaged spiritually, emotionally, and physically by addictions of any kind can find acceptance and understanding from the Word of God. They would receive from those who would compassionately communicate God's love, acceptance, and comfort out of their own testimonies.

Those who have experienced God's great mercy and grace are the very ones He will use as His ambassadors of healing and hope. After all, Jesus told His disciples they were to, "Go into all the world and preach the good news to all creation" (Mark 16:15 NIV). When the disciples did what He had asked them to do, "The Lord worked with them and confirmed his word by the signs that accompanied it" (Mark 16:20 NIV).

What is your testimony of the good news He has done in your life? Who have you shared your testimony with?
Begin to think of those you know who need to hear this good news! Look for opportunities to share God's love!

Day 7
Transparent Testimony

Joseph told his brothers, "But as for you, you meant evil against me; but God meant it for good, in order to bring it about as it is this day, to save many people alive."
-Genesis 50:20

I started by sharing my testimony in a small group setting. I began to be transparent about my own short comings. That freedom of not having to be perfect and not having to have it all together was so freeing, I could have shouted from the roof tops and sometimes I did. The Lord was really starting to show me what it meant to be free. By sharing my burdens and be being open and honest, I was able to help others share their burdens.

If only I had known to be transparent, I could have been spared a multiple of wounds to my spirit and soul.

Now I can honestly thank God for every wound I have because He will not waste a wound once it has been healed. He will use it to bring glory to His name. God was not the cause of any of my wounds, yet certainly, at times I blamed Him for many of them. However, when I began taking responsibility for my own wounds through my transparency, He was able to turn the wounds to good.

It may be that God is going to use the testimony of this book to deliver many of His people out of the bondages of their hurts, habits, and addictions. That is my prayer.

* *Use your journal to begin to write your own testimony.*
* *Write about how this book helped you begin your journey out of bondage.*
* *Be willing to be transparent and watch God use you to bring healing and hope to many that need to hear your story of God's love, acceptance, and healing.*

Conclusion
The Forty-Day Fast

Is not the fast that I have chosen: To loose the bonds of wickedness, to undo the heavy burdens, to let the oppressed go free, and that you break up every yoke?
Then your light shall break forth like the morning.
Your healing shall spring forth speedily, and your righteousness shall go before you:
The glory of the Lord shall be your rear guard.
Then shall you call, and the Lord will answer; you shall cry, and He will say, here I am.
(Isaiah 58:6, 8-9 NKJV)

Jesus said to His disciples, "However, this kind does not go out except by prayer and fasting" (Matthew 17:21).

From the beginning of November until early December, I prayed about doing a forty-day fast. Not knowing anything about doing an extended fast, but believing God was calling me to one I bought Dr. Towns' book, "Fasting for Spiritual Break Through." I ended up devouring the book and knew long before I finished it that God was definitely calling me to a forty-day fast. I had a piece of apple at 4:30 p.m. on Christmas day and officially started my fast.

I purposed in my heart to keep this fast and I believed God would make it supernatural in ways I may not understand. I also realized God may change my focus as I fasted so I wrote down five types of fasts out of nine that were in Dr. Towns' book that I believed were the purposes for my fast. They were the Disciples' fast, the Ezra fast, the Samuel fast, the Elijah fast, and the St. Paul fast. I listed separately under each heading the specific things I was fasting for, and the day I ended my fast I read all my concerns and was able to write down the reasons I fasted.

The Disciples' Fast led me to pray and fast for the yoke of lust in me to be completely broken so I could fully take His yoke upon me. Happily He performed that miracle for me and now I am no more tempted than other man and a whole lot less as well as a lot more cautious than most men. This fast took a lot of discipline and caused me to support it with lots of prayer.

The Ezra Fast was to relieve financial pressures especially while attending Liberty University full time so I would not have to work anymore than forty hours. I also fasted to purchase a house for my daughter and I so we could get out of apartment living. A lot of obstacles came up, but I kept going back to the throne of God believing this was something He had called me to fast for as well. I reminded Him I was seeking to do His will and glorify Him in my finances. My financial pressures have seemed to ease, yet I am not making any more money, only trying to be more careful with what I have. The day before I ended my fast, the deal went through for the modular home and I signed the papers. In a few months we will have our own home.

The Samuel Fast was to get opportunities to preach so I could share my passion for purity and lead others by example to the freedom I found in Christ from sexual sin, alcohol, drugs, food, religion, and unhealthy relationships. Shortly after I started my fast, I was invited to preach at the Chestnut Grove Baptist Church. On the twenty-second day of my fast, I preached at this small country black church that was full of love and totally blessed my heart. The spirit of worship at the Chestnut Grove Baptist church was amazing, and though I preached for an hour they seemed to want more.

On the seventeenth day of the fast, I was invited to be the speaker at a retreat for the North Carolina Korean Presbyterian Church. There were about eighty-five members who attend Duke University, North Carolina State, and UNC. They planned on meeting for three days of worship. They were joined by eleven Liberty University students. The retreat was titled. "True Worshippers; Seeking God's face not just His hands" and kicked off Friday, January 28, 2005, which was the thirty-fourth day of my fast. God's timing is never a coincidence.

I preached the first night for an hour and a half in a cold room while the congregation sat on cold, hard metal chairs. I preached again the next morning after we had corporate prayer and devotions. They then had their breakfast for another hour and a half. By then I really sensed God was doing something, so when I was given a few hours to relax I decided to go back to my room and pray and rest. After a season of prayer, I felt the need to rest so I lay down and slept for a half an hour, waking up refreshed, and hungering for God.

I spread my evening message on the floor and prostrated myself before God seeking His face and blessing on the message to be preached. As so often happens when I feel the presence of God strongly, tears started to flow. There is something about His love and holiness that is expressed in grace that breaks me continually. I got up knowing God was going to use me that night. I was confident He was planning on doing something, but I did not know what. I called my prayer partner from Thomas Road Baptist Church and asked Charlie to pray because I sensed God was really going to do something amazing that night.

The service went just like all of the others. I preached an hour and gave the invitation for salvation and recommitment just like all the other services. No hands went up for salvation but when asked for recommitment forty hands went up. Then I felt pressed in my spirit to call the people who raised their hands to confirm their convictions publicly so I backed up my portable pulpit and opened the altar. I was shocked to see people stream out of the chairs weeping and sobbing.

The front filled as did that sides and as I went around praying with those who had come forward with Pastor Moon. I noticed only a handful of people were left in their chairs and they were sitting there with bowed heads weeping.

Since that fateful day of my baptism in November of 1987, I have been preaching. My first sermon was from the baptismal pool with 3x5 cards as I shared my testimony for thirty minutes while standing in waist deep water. I have preached off and on ever since, but never have I seen God break so many people all at once by my sharing.

God certainly honors His word when we are obedient to a fast called by Him and is done for His glory.

The Elijah Fast was to change my core beliefs so I could remain completely free. "Then said Jesus to those Jews who believed Him, 'If you abide in my word, you are my disciples indeed. And you shall know the truth, and the truth shall make you free. Therefore if the Son makes you free, you shall be free indeed'" (John 8:31-32, 36). I began giving complete control over to the Lord and found myself tested again and again in regards to letting go of the control and keeping my hands off. I found it a truly liberating process and experience.

My mind was continually getting warped from the world system I lived in. I had not realized how much as I could not even see it even though I had been spending a few hours a day in prayer and Bible reading. During this fast, God showed me that was not enough to undo what a day of being in the world did to my thinking. I saw what a materialistic, wasteful, hedonistic culture I was living in. Then I realized it worse outside of the church because they did not have the Holy Spirit to convict them. Even without going to the movies, listening to secular music, reading secular writings or magazines or watching television except the news maybe once or twice a week, I had been brainwashed about what God had called me to do as a Christian.

Acts 18:22 says, "We must through many tribulations enter the kingdom of God." 2 Timothy 3:12 says, "Yes, and all who desire to live godly in Christ Jesus will suffer persecution." The mentality I had developed was not one of suffering but of prosperity and the pursuit of "The American Dream" with all of its pride and arrogance. I had asked God to try me, to search my heart, and show me the filth that was in me. When He began showing me this, I nearly got physically sick. In fact, at times as I fasted, I had to ask God to stop showing me how depraved I was because I could not take any more for a while.

No longer was I looking at others and comparing myself to them. I was looking at myself and comparing myself to His Son. If I was to follow anyone's example it would have to be His if I was to be completely free of all the yokes of bondage in me. Jesus said, "Take my yoke upon you and learn from Me, for I am gentle and lowly in heart" (Matthew 11:29).

As an American Christian, I was anything but gentle and lowly in heart. I was proud, self-sufficient, expectant, greedy, and always wanting more. As I took His yoke upon me and surrendered all my desires, goals, wants, and wishes, I found all my burdens lifted. He continually began applying the Word of God to change my thinking and now my core beliefs have been renewed.

I knew it was better to be humble than to be humiliated. I knew it was better to be transparent than be exposed.

The fifth and final reason for fasting was in the **St. Paul Fast**. I needed insight as I was trying to discern His will for me and make critical decisions at the same time. I realized a female friend I was deeply interested was not for me. It became clear helping others with soul and physical needs so they could be free in the spirit by sharing what I had gone through was His calling. He showed me He never wastes a wound given to Him. I am not sure when the ministry will begin or if I will have the spouse I desire to work alongside me, so I must stay faithful while waiting and being prepared.

"For the vision is yet for an appointed time; but at the end it will speak, and it will not lie. Though it tarries, wait for it; because it will surely come, it will not tarry" (Habakkuk 2:23). My vision was from God, so in His timing and by His power and provision it will come to pass. My responsibility is to just keep pressing on, keeping Him first in my life. I am to remain humble with a broken spirit and a broken and humble heart (Psalm 51:17).

It was such a blessing the day I ended my fast and read all these requests to see that God answered them all specifically as I had asked Him. Reading the whole journal I kept separate while fasting showed me all the things God had revealed to me during the fast. It showed me He knew right where I was and where I was going.

I left perfectionism in the dust, had every yoke broken, and was free to pursue His excellence as He revealed His perfect will for my life.

A renewed interest in short term missions stirred in me in part due to the Christianity I lived as an American which was making me ill and full of shame. I wondered what the founding religious fathers of the American faith would have thought of our Christianity now. I wondered what the martyrs of the reformation would have thought. I wondered what the Apostle Paul would have thought and said to address our culture and our modern-day Christianity.

The Apostle Paul said, "Labors more abundant, in stripes above measure, in prisons more frequently, in deaths often. From the Jews five times I received forty stripes minus one. Three times I was beaten with rods; once I was stoned; three times I was shipwrecked; a night and a day I have been in the deep; in journeys often, in perils of waters, In perils of robbers, in perils of my own countrymen, in perils of the gentiles, in perils in the city, in perils in the wilderness, in perils in the sea, in perils among false brethren; in weariness and toil, in sleeplessness often, in hunger and thirst in **fasting often** (emphasis mine), in cold and in nakedness—-besides the other things, which comes upon me daily; my deep concern for all the churches" (2 Corinthians 11:23-28 emphasis added).

I often wondered how an ordinary man could suffer so much and be used so greatly of God. The answer has to be for many reasons. He had an extraordinary conversion, but so do many of us today and down through the ages. He was led to the backside of the desert of Arabia as many of us are led to be apart from the world for a while so we can go back in and minister to the world in His strength. After taking off like a rocket with his zeal, God led him to a local assembly (Tarsus) where him was able to grow in grace as well as knowledge. Knowledge can come quickly and may accumulate rapidly, but grace takes decades to learn. Paul was called from a local church where he was ministering faithfully to the first mission trip of the early church.

Even in that he was not perfect. He still learning. Whatever the dissension was that arose between him and Barnabas over John Mark was later worked out as John Mark became profitable to him in the Ministry (Acts 15:36-41, 2 Timothy 4:11). Paul continued to be used greatly of God, fulfilling the very purpose God called him for (Acts 9:15) whether he knew what God revealed to Ananias or not. I believe God led Paul progressively even as He has led my beloved pastor, Dr. Jerry Falwell. The human mind and spirit cannot handle the wonderful thing God has in store for us when His sovereignty chooses to use us for His glory.

Dr. Falwell has said many times, "God uses you where you are, not where you ought to be."

I praise God that the Apostle Paul and Dr. Falwell did not make the mistakes I made especially in morality. I have had to accept and deal with my failures so I can say with them, "But by the grace of God I am what I am, and His grace toward me was not in vain; but I labored more abundantly than they all, yet not I, but the grace of God which was with me" (1 Corinthians 15:10).

This is being crucified with Christ, and this is definitely the lifestyle of Philippians 3:10, "that I may know Him and the power of His resurrection, and the fellowship of His sufferings, being conformed to His death."

I had to accept by His grace, I am what I am because my fall and my weaknesses led me to truly be crucified with Christ. This allowed His life, His death, and His resurrection power to shine through me so people only see Christ and not me. What is and has been suffering for me may not be suffering for other people and vice-versa. What is intense suffering for others may not be suffering at all for me because we are all individuals. God takes us right where we are and knows exactly what He has to do to accomplish His will in our lives. God knows what pressures to apply and when to apply them, as a precise gardener pruning to get the most fruit.

I am grateful that God has not judged America for its hedonistic, self-indulgent, proud, and materialistic ways with all its fleshly sins running rampant. I do not understand what stays His hand. It may be that there are many avenues the gospel light is spread from this land in spite of the carnality of a vast majority of believers.

Within most Christian churches whether big or small I believe there are "True Worshippers" who seek God's face through fasting and prayer, and just not His hands for what He can do for them. They realize they do not need things, they just need Him.

"If My people who are called by My name will humble themselves, and pray and seek My face and turn from their wicked ways, then I will hear from Heaven, and will forgive their sin and heal their land."
(2 Chronicles 7:14)

God knows in this world we will have tribulations from many causes (John 16:33) whether it is the world, the flesh or the devil (1 John 2:16). It is through much tribulation we will enter into the kingdom of God (Acts 14:22). All who will live godly in this present world will suffer in some form (2 Timothy 3:12).

However, to God goes all the glory because He has overcome the world through His Son, Jesus Christ (John 16:33). He is using every means possible to build our character to be conformed to the image of His Son.

It has been said many times God is more interested in our character than in our comfort and to that I say, "Amen!"

"May the grace of our Lord Jesus Christ be with you all as you work through the hurts, habits, and hang-ups that hinder your walk with Jesus Christ. May you truly be able to lay aside every weight that so easily ensnares us all." (Hebrews 12:1).

Appendix 1
My Testimony

In an effort to bring healing to male readers dealing with sexual sin, I have included my full testimony here.

Falling to Grace

June 6, 2004

I grew up in rural Maine in a typical dysfunctional home of a single parent. In spite of the fact that my mother was an adult child of an alcoholic not in recovery and both my grandmothers were widows, it was a close knit family. There was a lot of love, but also a lot of confusion. My parents divorced when I was eighteen months old. My dad moved to Oregon my mom stayed in Maine. I only met my dad twice, once when I was about six and again around eight years old. There were no birthday cards, letters or phone calls. He had a new family and I was not a part of it.

My step-father came into my life when I was around three years old, left us when I was around four, came back again when I was around nine, and left again one day while I was at school at the age of eleven. I was seventeen before I found out the truth of why my step-father left.

He was actually a family man with morals who won my trust. He brought us to church and cared for us, providing for our needs and being there for us, but he had one flaw. He was a thief. I found this out by accident overhearing my mother's phone call. Against her will, I went to the state prison to see him.

Around the age of six, I was exposed pornographic movies by some older cousins who knew how to run their dad's projector. There were six of us and none of us had reached puberty, yet we tried acting out what we had seen on the screen, to no avail. It was my first exposure to what I thought was love, intimacy, and acceptance.

Over the next few years we moved quite a bit. I was exposed to a lot drinking, and was ridiculed as a child because of my coke-bottle glasses and I did not have a dad like the other kids. There was a lot of rage trapped in me.

I always remember wanting a dad like other boys and being able to have the money to do family things and take care of people. I guess I realized how poor we were in second grade when we went to the house of the poorest kid in my class that I knew of, for what I thought was to give to their needs only to have them give to us.

Things grew worse when my mother was placed in a psychiatric hospital to be treated for depression and we were forced to live with my grandmother, a very devout Christian, former Baptist converted to the Nazarene. We went to church every Sunday and I started to feel accepted but then my mom got better and we lived with her and went to a Baptist-like community church. That was about when my step-father popped back in and we went to the Church of God for about eighteen months.

Throughout this time I would also go to Catholic mass with my other grandmother occasionally. God was real to me, but I did not know Him personally because I was confused by all the Christians convinced their way was the only right way of true worship.

Trying to Fill the God Void

The summer I turned 10 I had made an empty emotional profession of faith at a Church of God youth camp as I did not want to be left behind when Christ came, but I did not know Him. There was a superficial change that lasted about three days when I sang spiritual songs and talked of Jesus. However, after a fight with my younger brother spiritual singing stopped. My step-father tried to help me but to no avail and the following Spring he left for good.

At eleven after my step father had left, the same two older cousins who had exposed me to pornography had a keg party where I found what was to be my god for the next eleven years. I had my first of literally hundreds of partial or total blackout drunks.

My mother's remedy was to send me to Sunday school and church with my grandmother.

When I was twelve my cousins who had the keg party, punished me and their younger brother for pulling up their marijuana plants and turning them into their mother by making us smoke a joint. Like alcohol, I was addicted from the very first puff and had another lover to fill that void that is meant for God alone.

At the end of sixth grade, I skipped school with my cousin, his girlfriend, two female cousins, and an older girl I had a crush on. This girl sat on my lap and began kissing and fondling me, which I unfortunately began to enjoy. She acted this way so that my two cousins could sneak up on me, grab my pant legs and begin to strip me. I screamed for my male cousin to come help me, but his girlfriend was in on the plot saying they were just teasing me. As I lay on the floor, stripped from the waist down, the girls started to point and laughed hysterically. The shame was immense, but the desire for revenge was even greater. I knew someday I would show them I was not to be laughed at.

At the age of thirteen, I rebelled against the church. I only went to youth group fun things as I immersed myself deeper into drugs, alcohol, fantasy, and occasionally pornography. These were the people I seemed to fit in with. Regardless of their family background, we had this escapism together.

I was extremely shy by nature, fair at sports, and excelled in scholastics. My mother was busy with her own life, so I felt I was completely abandoned to find my own way. Whether in school, sports or partying, I was isolated among the crowd, always alone. I never got too close to anyone because I figured if I did they would not like me and I would lose what I had.

At the age of sixteen, I felt I had isolated even my drinking buddies and tried suicide by swallowing a bottle of aspirin and every other pill I could find. By the grace of God, my mom came home, read my suicide note, and got me to the hospital in time to have my stomach pumped. She turned to the local pastor for counsel, who in turn counseled me before I went to the west coast to live with my dad I had only met twice.

After I left, Pastor Evans told my mom he had never seen a battle between good and evil as strong as what was going on within me. He told her only prayer would help, but even though she did pray, I got worse.

Alcohol, Drugs, and Playboy Magazines

My move to Washington to live with my dad during my sophomore year allowed me to meet my step-brother who was an addict and a school dropout. He introduced me to the richest kid in town whose dad happened to be one of the biggest cocaine dealers in the northwest. This opened up a whole new world to me.

I went from an honor roll student to dropping out of school. My new best friend's dad had Playboy magazines all over the house and they did not seem to bother his wife. I became obsessed with looking at the magazines when I was sober enough to think of women. Those models became my ideals. I became lost in a realm of delusion and fantasy.

I explored other drugs with cocaine, like hallucinogenic mushrooms, LSD, and amphetamines. Before the end of that year, I had completely lost whatever sense I had of God and myself. I took a bus back to Maine which was just another move in a long list to try to fix me by trying another location. However, I found I took myself along wherever I went and eventually I would come out.

I finished high school by taking two years in one and then went to college for another location fix. My life continued to spiral downward. My roommates were drug addicts and alcoholics. I was sexually attacked by a senior under the guise of going to get drugs. By the time I made it back to the dorm, it looked like I had fought the entire football team, which was the lie I used to cover up the shame I felt for the rape.

I was expelled from the school for using drugs and vandalism. I decided the military was what I needed to get straight so I joined the army. Again, I excelled in the beginning scholastically as well as physically, always driving to be the best and to be at the top of the class. I got promoted before anyone in my battalion overseas. I was demoted the same day for failing a drug test. After fourteen months, I was discharged as a drug and alcohol rehabilitation failure, and written off as a hopeless case.

Drugs, Alcohol, and Sex

My next escape involved getting into relationships. When I worked as a traveling roofer I became a womanizer. Women were attracted to my physique. After a few months, I was struck by a car in New Hampshire and was hospitalized. I wrote to three women I had been involved with at that time. But I had put the wrong letters in two envelopes and ended up with one of the three. She came to live with me in 1986 and another fix was started. My drinking started again after about three months.

I turned the blame around to her and told her the problem was she was not a Christian and she need to be saved. Soon after she did profess to know Christ and we married. My drinking continued until one day after buying a six pack of beer and a pint of whiskey, I challenged God. If He was real, He would not let me get drunk. When I got drunk at the age of twenty-two, I felt for the first time that there was no God.

I Needed Help!

My life became total chaos and knew I needed help. I went through an in-patient drug and alcohol treatment center for three and a half weeks. I came out sober and seeking God, but only knew about the Alcoholics Anonymous. I took over an A.A. group and, like always, I began to excel, but I felt spiritually empty.

I left my wife and was going to file for a divorce when I heard Billy Graham preaching on the radio. As he read Ephesians 2:8-9, I realized that I was not really saved even though I always thought I was. I asked Jesus to forgive me of my sins and to be my Savior right there as I dropped to my knees. I asked Him to come into my life and change me because I could not do it.

I got back together with my wife, joined a small Bible preaching church, and was really growing in the Lord. The pastor took me under his wing and began mentoring me. He helped me focus on Christ by memorizing scripture, holding me accountable, and meeting with me weekly in counseling.

Unfortunately, the church forced him to resign nine months later because he took a strong stand against divorced men serving as deacons. I felt that I was being abandoned again. We found a nearby sister church, which was even more fundamental. Initially, I really grew and began to teach as well as preach in the pastor's absence, at nursing homes, and doing pulpit supply for other churches. I was appointed as a deacon at twenty-three and an elder at twenty-four though I had only been saved for two years.

Opening the Door Just a Crack

Shortly after our second child was born, my wife stopped attending church regularly, then hardly attended at all. I covered up for her while bringing the kids to church with me. As my wife became more liberal, I grew more legalist. On our tenth wedding anniversary, my wife suggested cocktails. I had been sober for about ten years and I thought if other Christians could drink so could I. After all, even Jesus drank wine (not knowing there was a huge difference in the wine of Christ's day and wine today.)

In my harsh legalism I viewed my alcoholism as a sin problem (which it is), but not a progressive disease (which it also is.) In less than a month, I was having black out drunks again. After our anniversary I got addicted to the bodybuilding lifestyle and admiring the fitness models that came with it which my could not compete with so she bought me a subscription to Playboy magazine.

The next five years were periods of repentance and backsliding leading me to committing adultery in November of 1997. Any hope I ever had of my wife returning to the Lord with me vanished. We stayed together and moved to Georgia where she had her first affair. My solution when I found out was to take a whole bottle of sleeping pills, a bottle of wine, and lead the police on a high-speed pursuit. I was taken to the emergency room, had my stomach pumped, and at the age of thirty-three, I was treated by a Psychiatrist for depression for six months.

The joy I had at salvation from being delivered from all my sins was gone and lust consumed me. I visited a couple of sleazy massage parlors, hired a couple of exotic dancers, and had several emotional affairs where there was no physical contact, just flirting and robbing my wife of my heart.

My wife began having multiple affairs, left me and our kids once for a few months, and then for good in 2001. Her last affair led her to filing for divorce and she left us for good September 11, 2001. I was broken, but not enough. I prayed for her to come back for over five months, and was faithful to my Church.

Then I stumbled in my own affair with a married coworker. When I confessed my sin to my Pastor in Maine, the church's response was to forbid me to speak or pray at church. I could not share testimony of God's love or the insight He gave me from His Word as God began healing me in my brokenness.

It was the worse experience of my life, but I was held by the cords of my own sin. I fled Maine to Florida in 2002, but I was not strong enough to break the ties, so after a few months the married woman came to Florida. For two months, I sank deeper into depression with the thoughts of suicide often returning. The Lord, who in His sovereignty has watched over my entire life, reached down and removed this woman back to Maine with her husband.

Seeking Counsel

I sought help for what I thought was sexual addiction because of my lusting for women. I was told by Christians and non-Christians alike that everyone looks. This warped sense of thinking led me to my final episode with a woman I befriended through work who came to my house and performed oral sex on me.

That is when I knew, no matter what the world, my counselors or Christian peers said, I must do everything I could to stay pure. My desires had led me to lust, my lust had blinded me to sin, and my sin hardened my heart so that I could not see sin as a sin.

That realization was the final straw. It has been a long and very hard road to recovery filled with many ups and downs. I have battled depression, loneliness, and temptations at every turn, but God has been faithful through it all.

I began looking for churches in Vero Beach. Going from church to church filling out the visitor's card and requesting a visit from the pastor was to no avail, not even a phone call or card. Then I visited Kings Baptist Church. The day after filling out the card, Dr. Russell Vickery, senior pastor, was in my living room. I poured out all my poison in detail and all I sensed was love, acceptance, and compassion.

The first comment he made was about my former church was, "They really stoned you!"

The next night a deacon and Sunday school teacher showed up so I did the same thing and got the same response. I joined the church and they loved me just as I was right back into fellowship. The Lord truly used that church to heal me of many of my hurts.

Three months later I was teaching multiple adult Sunday school classes, leading council time for Awana, and singing in the choir. During my family devotions in February of 2003, I told God I could not live the Christian life, so I was going to quit trying. The Lord responded, "Good, now My Son can live His life through you." Galatians 2:20 became a reality, not just a verse.

A few months later, I sensed the Lord calling me to the Baptist College of Florida. This led to a tear filled, sobbing argument where I told God I was divorced, had fallen into immorality as His child, was disqualified from the ministry, and was a single dad on top of it all. However, I surrendered and told God my faith was small, but if He opened the doors I would walk through them.

The love, acceptance, forgiveness, and peace I experienced broke me like nothing I had ever experienced before, which truly proves it is God's goodness that leads to repentance, not His judgment. With all my heart, my course was set for I knew what was in me, a desperately wicked and deceitful heart, and I gave it all to Him to use as He saw fit, regardless of the cost.

The last challenge He gave me that afternoon was Matthew 10:37-39, "He who loves father or mother more than Me is not worthy of Me. And he who does not take his cross and follow after Me is not worthy of Me. He who finds his life shall lose it, and he who loses his life for My sake shall find it." The Lord then asked if I would be willing to give up my children for Him. My answer was yes, I trusted Him that much.

After spending the summer with their mother, my kids decided to stay in Maine with her and her boyfriend. It rocked my faith to its foundation, but I sought counsel and kept my eyes on Him knowing He had a reason.

My Testimony

Thus began a series of miracles that got me to the Baptist College of Florida, pastoring a church, attending Liberty University, and a ministry to shut-ins. So many miracles and supernatural provisions have continued to this day that it would take hours to list.

I know Romans 11:29, "The gifts and callings of God are without repentance." I have always known I was called as a preacher, and as I have exercised spiritually I have discerned my other spiritual gifts. Every spiritual test I have taken confirms these gifts: Preacher–# 1 *Kerusso*, to herald, to proclaim with practical application, #2 teaching, clear explanation producing spiritual growth, and #3 Shepherding, leading, guiding, and nurturing people in their faith. The next two often flip flop depending on the test: Exhortation–empathy, encouragement and support. Discernment–distinguishing between truth and error, pure and impure motives.

It took four to six months of prayer and weekly fasting (one to two days a week) to discern how God wanted me to use my gifts for His glory. My heart is still open to His leading because every time I think I have it figured out He moves me in a new direction. Each time complementing and building from the other directions He has led, but still different. I have always known God wants to use me as a preacher and teacher, but counseling and writing have kind of developed since I returned to the Lord.

I have been seeking to stay balanced and sensitive to God while working toward these goals and actively seeking Him. I have never seen in scripture where He called us to be idle. I have learned the best gift is availability. The Lord still loves me enough to show me my selfishness, my self-centeredness, the lust that is in me, the impurity, the pride, and self-sufficiency just to list a few. But as I see it, repent, and cry out for His cleansing I am healed. As I surrender it all to Christ, confessing my sins and laying my addictions at the foot of the cross, I realize the power of every sin and addiction is broken. However, I need to leave it at the cross where the victory was won for me.

At the present I am not struggling with any addictions, but the battles will always be there. Sin and addiction are both the absence of God from some part of my life, so He helps me see where I have shut Him out and the power of that sin/addiction is broken.

Remembering Psalm 37:4-5, 73:25, and Matthew 6:33 help me to keep Christ first, as does a few close accountability partners I feel safe being absolutely transparent with. Though we stumble we shall not be utterly cast down, for the Lord upholds us with his hand Psalm 37:24. James 5:16 tells us to confess our faults one to another that we may healed, while Hebrews 10:24-25 tells us to consider one another and to stir one another up to good works and not to forsake the assembling of ourselves together, no Lone Ranger Christians.

Backsliding is the worst of all sins imaginable. 2 Peter 2:21-23 says it is better to have not known the right way than to turn from it for the dog will return to his vomit and the pig to the mire. Thankfully, God's grace and mercy extends even there so that I can see sanctification is a process with perfection being the end result. Though I strive to that end, I know in this life I am only to press toward that mark. The final product, like the start is His completely (Philippians 1:6).

If God can restore me (and He did) for the upward calling in Christ Jesus, then I know He can heal and restore anyone. May the Holy Spirit of God take His Word throughout this book to bring conviction and repentance to those who need it May my testimony bring comfort and hope for those who are in the struggle (2 Corinthians 1:4).

About the Author

I grew up in rural Maine and attended various church denominations which led to confusion. As an early teen, I was exposed to drugs, alcohol, and pornography which became my idols until I met Jesus Christ at age twenty-two.

For a few years everything was wonderful but legalism slowly crept in killing my joy, maiming my love for Christ and destroying my walk with the Lord until I fell so far into a horrible pit that the only way out was grace. I found myself truly experiencing Jesus' life-giving and freeing grace.

Appendix 2
Other References

1. Dr. Elmer Towns, *Fasting for Spiritual Break Through*.

2. The first and best book I read on as a person coming out of sexual addiction was, *At the Altar of Sexual Idolatry* by Steve Gallagher because of its biblical content. It is a powerful and comprehensive examination of a person trapped in the bondage of sexual sin. His latest book is just as powerful because he has a compassionate heart and dedication to help men overcome sexual sin through the application of the Bible.

3. *Every Man's Battle* by Stephen Arteberg, Fred Stoeker, and Mike Yorkey lists twenty separate references in the New Testament for sexual purity that is not exhaustive.

4. *The Final Freedom* by Douglas Weiss, Ph.D. gives a lot of practical steps and some tremendous insight to the biological and psychological aspects of the addiction. This was another key issue for me in understanding the addiction aspect and what was going on with my body. There were some definite things I needed to know about the cycles every male body goes through that would not be understood or fixed by reading the bible

more or praying more, which is the typical answer you get from a narrow minded fundamentalist.

5. The classic book on sexual addiction, *Out of the Shadows Understanding Sexual Addiction* by Patrick Carnes, PHD. takes you inside the mind of the sex addict and you learn it is not different than any other addiction, it just has different manifestations. Carnes gives no indication of being a Christian, nor does his book, but the volume of cases alone that he has seen in this field gives tremendous insight into what happens to the addict as they delve into the addiction. From his description of the trance like state an addict goes into just prior to acting out to the processes inside the mind.

6. Dr. Mark R. Laaser, *Healing the Wounds of Sexual Addiction*, speaks of an abstinence contract, "It is virtually important for sex addicts to stop all sexual behaviors for at least ninety days." According to Laaser, "Abstinence reverses the sex addict's core belief that 'Sex in my most important need.' Instead, the sex addict discovers 'Sex is *not* my most important need.'"